education of the severely/profoundly handicapped:

what is the least restrictive alternative?

by
n. dale gentry
university of idaho

a. lee parks
university of idaho

thomas n. fairchild
series editor

danial b. fairchild
illustrator

LEARNING CONCEPTS
2501 N. Lamar Austin, Texas 78705 (512) 474-6911

Library of Congress Cataloging in Publication Data

Gentry, N Dale.
    Education of the severely/profoundly handicapped.

    (Mainstreaming series)
    1. Mentally handicapped children—Education.
2. Mentally handicapped children—Care and treatment.
I. Parks, A. Lee, joint author. II. Title.
LC4601.G28   371.9'28   77-13515
ISBN 0-89384-029-7

Learning Concepts
2501 North Lamar
Austin, Texas 78705

To my mother, Lois Parks, for her concern for people.

—Lee Parks

To Pat, Dennis, Paul and Mona.

—Dale Gentry

acknowledgements

The authors wish to express thanks to several people who have directly or indirectly assisted in the development of this manuscript. At the University of Washington, we wish to thank Georgia Adams, Bob Crebo, Les Hazel, Susan Joslyn, Dennis Mithany and Susan Zylstree. Their work with children has provided the case studies cited.

Lee Parks wishes to thank several people of The Ohio State University whose daily work with children has provided the basis for much of the text. In particular, we wish to thank Jean Berkwitt, Kathy Borchart, Deloris Frey, Mark Gearhartstein, Sherry Ireland, Robin Reid, and Karen Watson.

Thanks also to those who have provided cartoon ideas, critique, and typing. Thank you dear friends, Lee Brydon, Carolyn Fairchild, Sherri Newell, and Dr. "Feelgood."

preface

In the past, educational needs of exceptional children were met by removing them from the "mainstream" of the regular classrooms, and serving them in a variety of segregated, self-contained special classes. The trend in the '70's is educating exceptional children in the least restrictive educational setting; that is, as close as possible to their normal peers. This concept of "mainstreaming" exceptional children has received considerable support from within and outside the educational community. Although self-contained special classes will always be a meaningful alternative for some children, the personal and educational needs of many exceptional children can better be served in the regular class program with the supportive services of ancillary personnel and/or resource room help.

With the emphasis on "mainstreaming," the regular class teacher is now expected to meet the needs of exceptional children in his or her classroom along with all the other children in the class. The problem is that most regular class teachers have little or no preparation in the area of educating exceptional children. Regular class teachers need basic information regarding the various exceptionalities, and more specifically, practical suggestions which they can employ to enhance the "mainstreamed" exceptional child's personal and educational development.

The MAINSTREAMING SERIES was written to fill this need. Most of the books in the SERIES address themselves to specific areas of exceptionality, allowing teachers to select from the SERIES according to their interests or needs. The texts provide information designed to eliminate misconceptions and stereotypes and to improve the teacher's understanding of the exceptional child's uniqueness. Numerous practical suggestions are offered which will help the teacher work more effectively with the exceptional child in the "mainstream" of the regular classroom. Other texts in the SERIES focus on the public law supporting mainstreaming, individualized educational programs, and working with parents.

Currently, there is a great deal of controversy surrounding the use of categories and labels. The books in the SERIES are organized according to categories of exceptionality because the content within each book is only relevant for a specific handicapping condition. The intent is not to propagate labeling; in fact, labeling children is inconsistent with the philosophy of the SERIES. The books address themselves to behaviors and how teachers can work with these behaviors in exceptional children. The books in the SERIES are categorized—not the children. The books are categorized in order to cue teachers to the particular content for which they might be looking.

There is much truth in the old saying, "A picture is worth a thousand words." A cartoon format was used for each book in the MAINSTREAMING SERIES as a means of sustaining interest and emphasizing important concepts. The cartoon format also allows for easy, relaxed reading. We felt that teachers, being on the firing line all day, would be more likely to read and refer to our material, than to a lengthy text filled with theory and jargon. Typical to cartooning is the need to exaggerate, stereotype, and focus on our weaknesses. I sincerely hope the cartoons do not offend any children, parents, or professionals, because that is not the purpose for which they were intended. They are intended to help you think.

I hope you find this book helpful in your work with exceptional children, or with any other children, since they are all special.

THOMAS N. FAIRCHILD
SERIES EDITOR

contents

chapter 1

---

education of the severely/profoundly handicapped

HISTORICAL PERSPECTIVE

Among the general population, there is a large number of individuals who can be referred to as severely/profoundly handicapped. They have also been called other things like severely retarded and multiply handicapped. Generally speaking, they are people who are unable to function independently. In the past, such persons were separated from the mainstream of American society. Many were placed in institutions for the retarded.

Professionals in the field believed residential institutions provided the most appropriate service for severely handicapped persons. Parents were advised that institutions provided better services than those available in the community. Unfortunately, this was often true, since few services were available in many communities.

The public schools did not have the teachers or curriculum needed to effectively serve severely handicapped children. The schools were mainly concerned with "educating" children in the "3 R's."

4

School age children lacking pre-academic skills were frequently viewed as un-educable. Such children were referred to as "trainable" or even "sub-trainable."

Unfortunately, those who were classified as "trainable" or considered lower functioning were not trained. They were often placed in custodial settings.

Management programs for residents were often neglected and generally confined to those skills that made care easier. Training for greater independence was rare.

All varieties of persons were housed in this sort of institutional setting. Some appeared to be mentally retarded; some had physical problems like cerebral palsy or sensory deficits; others were emotionally disturbed. In many cases, etiology was unknown. Often individuals had several handicaps.

DEFINITIONS

Who are the severely handicapped? Many assume that they are vegetables who are bedridden and unable to survive without intensive care.

Actually the severely handicapped are a very heterogeneous group. In fact, as yet there is no single common definition that is accepted by most states.

The definition used by the Bureau for the Education for the Handicapped (BEH) is not uniformly adopted by each state. However, let's begin by examining this definition.

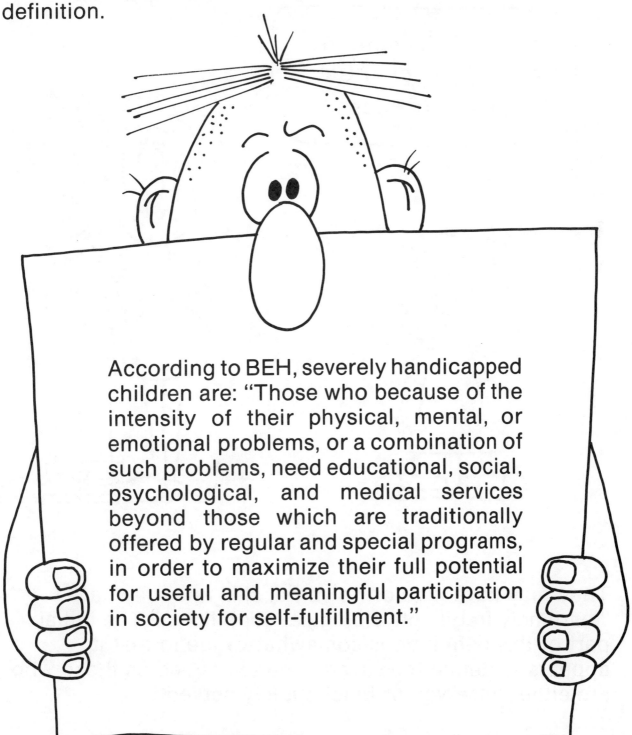

According to BEH, severely handicapped children are: "Those who because of the intensity of their physical, mental, or emotional problems, or a combination of such problems, need educational, social, psychological, and medical services beyond those which are traditionally offered by regular and special programs, in order to maximize their full potential for useful and meaningful participation in society for self-fulfillment."

They may engage in behaviors like self-stimulation, self-mutilation and temper tantrums.

Isn't Lee turning a pretty shade of blue? Matches his eyes.

They may have little or no verbal skill and may have "extremely fragile physiological conditions." The initial part of this definition is somewhat vague in that it appears to define the severely handicapped as those who are either unserved or inadequately served.

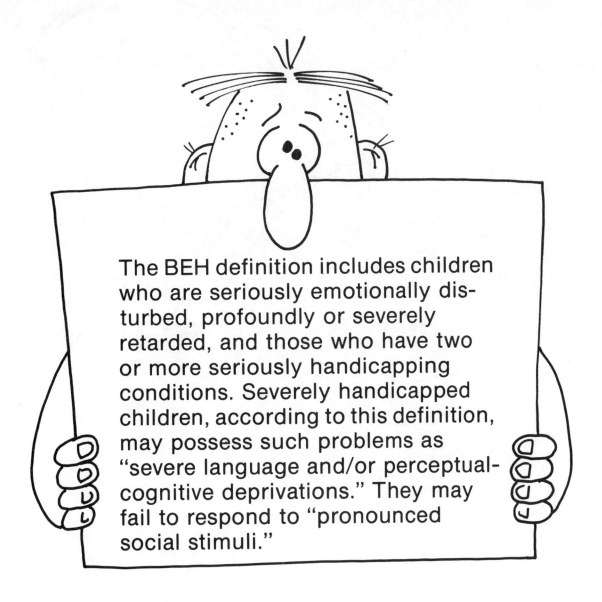

The BEH definition includes children who are seriously emotionally disturbed, profoundly or severely retarded, and those who have two or more seriously handicapping conditions. Severely handicapped children, according to this definition, may possess such problems as "severe language and/or perceptual-cognitive deprivations." They may fail to respond to "pronounced social stimuli."

Some states use definitions that refer primarily to mental retardation. Others consider multiple handicaps as constituting a severe handicap. Some consider that one or more of the handicaps should be severe. Others include those persons who have traditionally been considered as "trainable."

For the purposes of this book, the BEH definition will be accepted. Since there is such a large group of children in the trainable classification who are receiving inadequate services, that population will be included also. In reality, most classrooms for the severely handicapped include children who are in the trainable category. This is especially true in small towns and rural areas.

The curriculum and the teaching procedures discussed in this book address those children who possess one or more of the following problems: (1) non-ambulatory and/ or other severe motor problems, (2) lack of academic skills, (3) little or no verbal skill, (4) self- stimulation and/or self-mutilation, (5) lack of self-care skills such as feeding, toileting, and grooming.

It will include children who may be labeled as severely or moderately retarded, emotionally disturbed and/or physically handicapped.

TRENDS IN SERVICE

Though children with severe handicaps have historically not received services, and in many cases have been shut away from society, this trend is clearly changing. Because of sweeping reforms in state and national legislation and litigation, services are being provided to ever greater numbers of children each year.

The development of the National Association for Retarded Citizens (NARC) in 1950 was significant in bringing national attention to the retarded. As a result, new state and federal laws were passed. In the early 1960's President Kennedy's interest in the plight of the retarded provided a tremendous thrust to the general field of services for the handicapped. Resources became available for service, training, and research.

Public schools began to serve handicapped children. Where previously parent-operated programs were often all that were available, the public schools developed self-contained classes for handicapped children.

Pennsylvania Association for Retarded Citizens vs. Commonwealth of Pennsylvania (1971) was a landmark class action suit which mandated that all children, regardless of label or potential, be provided access to public educational services.

Though the decision in this case applied only to Pennsylvania, professionals knew that it would be only a matter of time until the same rights were extended to children in all states.

A recent legislative development is Public Law 94-142, *The Education for All Handicapped Children Act.* It is a federal law that insures a free and appropriate public education for all handicapped children. A major aspect of the law is that it requires children to be served in the least restrictive setting, which will be discussed in greater detail later in this chapter.

Parallel to the litigation-legislation trend has been the deinstitutionalization movement which was spurred by the President's Panel on Mental Retardation (1962). It strongly encouraged states to decentralize their institutions by placing residents in smaller units closer to their natural homes. Institutional programs have made advances similar in at least one respect to those of the public schools; that is, to provide services in the least restrictive setting.

Institutionalization should be only one of several options available to a severely handicapped individual. It should be one service in a continuum of services—not a dead-end placement from which the person can, for all practical purposes, never return.

All individuals who are institutionalized have a right to treatment and to progress to less restrictive settings. They cannot be conveniently placed away from society without services.

The handicapped individual's right to treatment was established in the case of *Wyatt vs. Stickney* in Alabama. Among other findings, this case established that each resident of the institution must have an individualized treatment program as well as a humane physical and psychological environment in which to live.

The court also ruled that each institutionalized resident should be served in the least restrictive setting necessary for treatment to be provided.

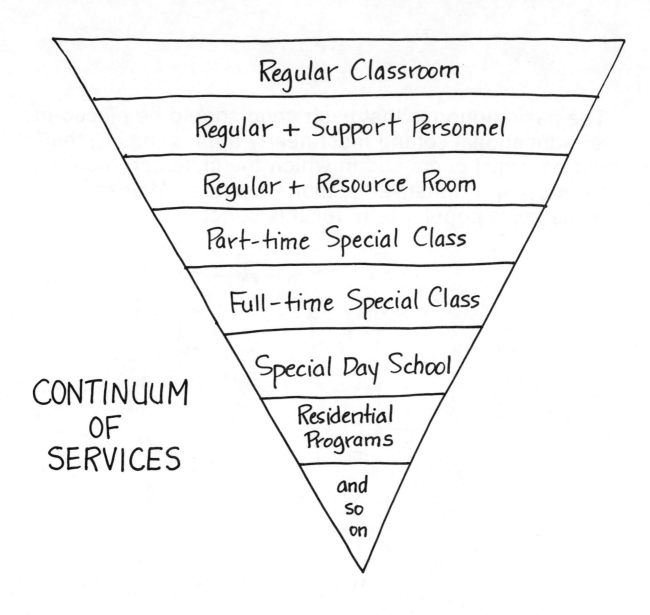

Regular Classroom

Regular + Support Personnel

Regular + Resource Room

Part-time Special Class

Full-time Special Class

Special Day School

Residential Programs

and so on

CONTINUUM OF SERVICES

LEAST RESTRICTIVE SETTING

Courts in several states have ruled that education for the handicapped be provided in the "least restrictive setting." The concept was first ordered in the Pennsylvania case; it was incorporated into Federal law in 1974. More recently, it has become an integral part of Public Law 94-142.

The basic notion is that each child should be placed in an educational setting most nearly approximating that of more normal peers and in which the child can receive the most appropriate educational services. *Mainstreaming* is the more popular term for this concept.

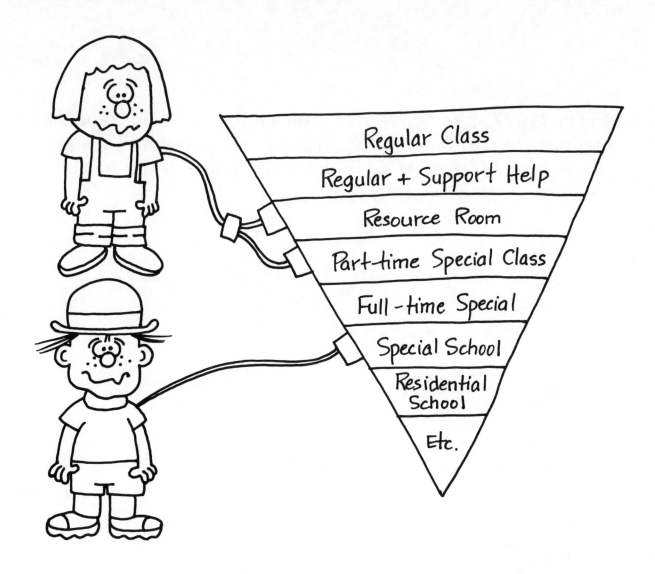

Contrary to what many believe, mainstreaming does not necessarily mean placing a handicapped child in the regular classroom. The least restrictive alternative refers to a continuum of services making it possible for a child to be educated in the setting where his/her needs can best be served while also insuring that he/she will not be *unduly* restricted. Should services in a setting become inappropriate because of behavioral development or regression, it provides that alternative settings and programs will be sought.

Edgar (1977) has presented guidelines to assist teachers and parents of severely handicapped children in determining the least restrictive alternative in educational programs. In *examining facilities* ...

...parents and teachers should ask whether or not the child has been placed in a physical environment that is as close as possible to the mainstream of community life.

A second factor to consider is the extent to which the physical facility isolates the child from other children as well as from adults. And, are support services like physical therapy and medical services available to the child in the classroom?

Parents and teachers should also look at the child's *opportunities for normal integration.* Children should be in settings where they are able to practice, in real life situations, the skills they have learned.

They should also have the opportunity to interact with less handicapped as well as normal peers. Where possible, these opportunities should be a regular part of each school day.

Appropriate educational programming is the third major aspect of a least restrictive alternative as discussed by Edgar (1977). The child should have access to a professional staff. The staff should be appropriately trained, use proper assessment procedures and training techniques, and provide ongoing evaluation of the child's performance.

If parents and teachers consider such aspects of a child's program, they will increase the likelihood of providing an appropriate education in the least restrictive setting for the child. They must always keep in mind that the child should move away from the mainstream of community life only as far as is necessary. The child should then return toward that mainstream as quickly as possible. Moves in either direction must be supported with data.

chapter 2

---

assessment and curriculum

INTRODUCTION

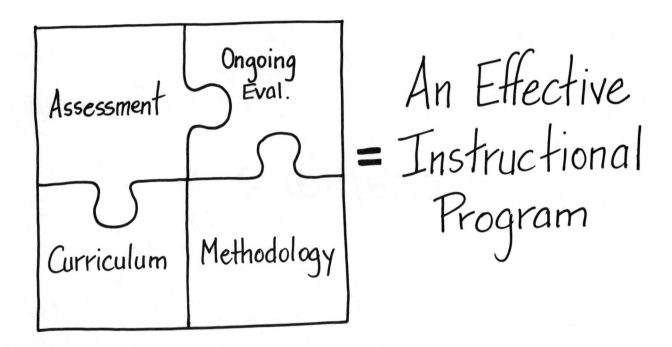

There are several components to an effective instructional program. Though various professionals divide the problem differently, most identify at least four basic components. These are (1) assessment, (2) curriculum, (3) methodology, and (4) ongoing evaluation. This chapter presents information on the first two of these. Methodology and ongoing evaluation will be discussed in Chapter 3.

Assessment is usually seen as the beginning point in the various instructional models. There are a number of factors that need to be known before the teacher can actually start instruction with the child. The teacher needs to know whether there are any medical or physical factors that will limit performance or affect what should be taught and how it should be taught. Very importantly, the teacher also needs to know what capabilities the child possesses as well as the deficits and excesses demonstrated. Assessment tells us *what* needs to be done and sometimes tells us *how* it should be done. In the end, it helps determine whether or not we accomplished the development of skills we set out to achieve.

MEDICAL ASSESSMENT

Medical assessment is especially important for severely handicapped children. They have an endless variety of medical problems which need to be communicated to teachers and parents. However, we wish to caution parents and teachers about the use of labels and diagnosed syndromes; labels and syndromes do not in themselves provide information relevant for determining appropriate instruction.

Such information is only important if it indicates a limitation the teacher needs to work around or suggests an alternate instructional or management strategy. If the child has a heart problem the teacher must plan appropriate physical activities. If the child's tongue is excessively large in proportion to the mouth size or vice versa, that provides information to speech specialists about which sounds the child may have difficulty producing. But, by itself, knowing a child is Down's Syndrome is relatively unimportant.

Medical history can provide useful information about possible causes of handicapping conditions. Family medical history can provide information about handicapping conditions that may be the result of genetic disorders.

Birth history including pregnancy, labor and delivery information may also indicate causes of a handicap. Was there prolonged labor? Did the baby have problems getting breath? Were blood types compatible? Were Apgar scores low? (An Apgar is a measure of reactivity given to newborns). However, these possible causes—like labels—do not in themselves lead to appropriate treatment or accurate prognosis.

Assessment of physical growth is one of the most important early measures. School nurses and pediatricians often keep growth charts on children which can be used at a later time to reveal sudden increases or lags in development. They may also show significant deviations from the norm.

The physical examination usually measures vital signs such as temperature, blood pressure, pulse, and respiration rates. Results from examination of the skin can indicate early signs of blood or bone marrow diseases. Lesions in the skin may be early indicators of brain abnormalities. Head measures and facial features provide information about the possible existence of various syndromes.

Nervous system function is assessed by observing the way in which a child crawls, skips, and runs, the size of pupils and reaction to light, body balance, and response to stimuli like lights and sounds. Especially important are a variety of reflexive reactions which may indicate neurological impairments. Both parents and teachers can provide important information to the physician that will be helpful in assessing nervous system functioning.

Laboratory analyses provide information for diagnosis. These tests could include chromosome analysis; examination of blood and urine for abnormal amounts of sugar, fats, and amino acids; and hormone analysis. Examination of chromosomes is usually not advised unless the child exhibits physical abnormalities as well as low intellectual functioning.

It is important to remember that diagnosis, by itself, does not necessarily provide educationally useful information. Parents and teachers must be careful not to expect that diagnostic information will automatically lead to the development of programs for the child.

EDUCATIONAL ASSESSMENT

Educational assessment is probably the most usable information collected on a child. As before, it should not be used for categorizing alone. Educational assessment should provide immediate data on pupil performance and provide a basis for long term evaluation. It should tell the teacher what skills the child has and does not have.

LIST of SKILLS

CAN PERFORM	CANNOT PERFORM
1. Spit six feet	1. Syllabication
2. Blow a 5 inch bubble	2. Fractions
3. Eat a live nightcrawler	

It is commonly accepted that it is most appropriate to begin instruction at the point where the child can function. The point at which failure occurs in a list of sequenced skills is the point at which instruction should begin. Thus, there should be a direct correlation between what is on the test and the curriculum content. The two should be inseparable.

Many of the newer assessments are called criterion-referenced tests. These are tests in which the child is compared to her/himself.

There is no norm (comparison) group. The items are stated in performance terms. The tests are often lengthy since, where possible, it is usually desirable to have all of the most critical behaviors (or skills) represented on the test. It is permissible and desirable to teach to the test. Many criterion-referenced tests tell not only *what* the child should do, but *how well* it should be done.

On the succeeding pages we will discuss a variety of assessments. Some will be criterion-referenced; some will be norm-referenced; in other cases it is difficult to classify them as either. All will be referred to as long-term assessments. Long-term assessment means any assessment that is not ongoing in nature—not done on a daily, weekly or bi-weekly basis. They are completed anywhere from once every other month to once a year. Short-term assessments will be considered in Chapter 3.

Long-term assessment should measure the child's performance in each of several areas of functioning. Sometimes this can be done with one test. Sometimes it requires the use of several. Information on some widely used tests is presented on the following pages, though the reader is strongly advised to consult local, state, and national educational resources for further information. All are classified as "educational" for purposes of the present chapter because they contain items that teachers can "teach to" in the class or community. As can be seen, the areas of importance to teachers of the severely handicapped cover a much broader range of skills than those for teachers of less involved children.

The *American Association on Mental Deficiency (AAMD) Adaptive Behavior Scale* is commonly used with severely handicapped individuals. Its general purpose is to measure one's ability to cope with the natural and social demands of day-to-day living. This is an important measure since it represents a basic indicator of whether or not an individual can be considered retarded. If adaptive behavior is not poor, then, according to the AAMD definition, a person is not retarded.

The Scale can be administered by a teacher who goes through the items one at a time and judges the extent to which a child does or does not display the behavior of concern for each of the test items. Two major areas are assessed—developmental skills and maladaptive behavior. The ten domains within the developmental area are: 1. independent functioning, 2. physical development, 3. economic activity, 4. language development, 5. numbers and time, 6. domestic activity, 7. vocational activity, 8. self-direction, 9. responsibility, and 10. socialization.

Fourteen domains are assessed in the maladaptive behavior area. These are: 1. violent and destructive behavior, 2. anti-social behavior, 3. rebellious behavior, 4. untrustworthy behavior, 5. withdrawal, 6. stereotyped behavior and odd mannerisms, 7. inappropriate interpersonal manners, 8. unacceptable vocal habits, 9. unacceptable or eccentric habits, 10. self-abusive behavior, 11. hyper-active tendencies, 12. sexually aberrant behavior, 13. psychological disturbances, and 14. use of medication.

Teachers can administer the scale, identify weak areas, and then prepare a program that will develop the identified skills. Later, the scale may be re-administered to determine the degree to which the program has been successful. Results can be useful to parents, principals, and other professional staff. Without such long-term assessment, we are often unable to determine a child's progress toward the larger end goal of increased independence for daily life functioning.

Another useful instrument to consider is the *Camelot Behavioral Checklist.* It was designed to identify areas of weakness in order that these weaknesses may be strengthened. The checklist is composed of 399 items, arranged in order of difficulty, into ten domains:

1. Self-help
2. Physical development
3. Home duties
4. Vocational development
5. Economic behavior
6. Independent travel
7. Numerical skills
8. Communication skills
9. Social behavior
10. Responsibility

The checklist is administered by one or more adults who are familiar with the current functioning of the child. If the teacher is not well acquainted with the child, the parent should be asked to assist in completing the assessment. Ideally, the parent should be involved under nearly all circumstances. Items are rated as "can do" and "needs training." After the assessment is completed, the teacher can begin preparing programs to develop skills the child needs. *A Skill Acquisition Program Bibliography* is available which provides a list of programs already developed for various behaviors on the checklist.

The *Portage Project Checklist* is another assessment that is appropriate for higher level severely handicapped children. It includes items that range in difficulty level from birth to age five. The areas it covers include:

1. Cognition
2. Self-help
3. Motor
4. Language
5. Socialization

Accompanying the checklist is a card file which provides suggested activities for developing the behaviors on the checklist. Each of the areas is color coded for more convenient reference. As each new skill is learned, the teacher dates the record form and progresses to the next higher level. Typically, the teacher targets deficits across curricular areas so that educational programs can be developed for two or three deficits simultaneously.

Other assessments are available in addition to the ones previously discussed. They are listed below but not discussed. Most of these assessments are adequate long-term measures. Teachers should carefully review an assessment before adopting it since the behaviors need to be as closely related to curriculum as possible. It is illogical to assess one thing and teach another.

Other tests that teachers may wish to review are:

- Balthazar Scales of Adaptive Behavior
- The YEMR and TMR Performance Profiles
- Cain-Levine Social Competence Scale
- The Vineland Social Maturity Scale
- Learning Accomplishment Profile
- Nebraska Client Progress System
- Pennsylvania Training Model
- The TARC Assessment System
- Student Progress Record
- System FORE

CURRICULUM

Conflicts have existed regarding what constituted appropriate curriculum for severely handicapped children.

Curriculum for the severely handicapped is considerably different from content areas traditionally taught in the public schools; the "3 R's" may never be a part of severely handicapped children's schooling.

Most professionals feel that curricula for the severely handicapped should contain skills for developmental levels through age six. Of course, this does not apply to certain self-care skills like shaving. These kinds of skills are included in the curriculum even though they are adult level items.

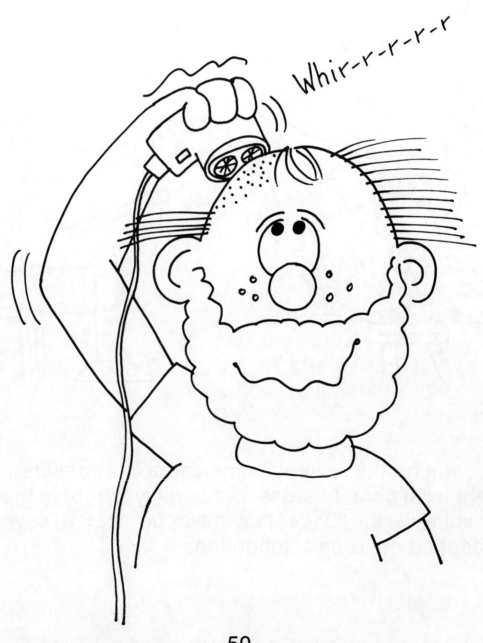

Whir-r-r-r-r

There are certain characteristics that a curriculum for the severely handicapped should incorporate; one is that it should be **functional.**

That is, it should teach the individual to do something that will be of most use considering the individual's limited repertoire of present and probable future skills. Given the trend in normalization, these skills should be useful in the general society beyond the training setting.

The curriculum should be **extensive,** ideally consisting of an exhaustive number of items within each curriculum area. These items should be stated in behavioral terms. Since it is probably impossible to develop an exhaustive list of behaviors, teachers should always view items as open-ended, so that skills can be added or modified as needed for each handicapped individual.

When necessary, a curriculum should incorporate **prosthetic options.** The motorically impaired child may require a sandwich holder in order to eat. Children with language difficulties often benefit from sign language. When these and other alternatives increase children's options they should be included.

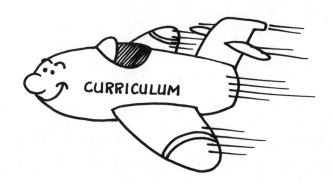

Another characteristic that a curriculum should have is a **data-base.** Each item should be validated. The ultimate question for each curriculum is, "Does it lead to the development of short and long range skills that are sought for that individual?"

Finally, as previously mentioned, the measurement system should correlate with the curriculum. We should teach and evaluate the same things. To do otherwise would be like going to the doctor with a cold and having him determine that your condition is improved when your athlete's foot disappears. Not to teach to the deficit of concern is similar to treating "around" the cold.

CURRICULAR AREAS

Curricular areas for the severely handicapped cover a wide range of skills. As the reader will see, education of the severely handicapped is clearly an interdisciplinary endeavor. When problems are small, there is relatively little need for multiple disciplines to become involved. A team of experts is not needed to help a normal child learn new math facts. Yet, for the severely handicapped the problems can be enormous, and in many cases the answers are not yet known. In a manner of speaking, when we work with such a child, we are going somewhere we have never been before.

The curriculum for the severely handicapped commonly includes the following general skill areas:

- Self-care
- Socialization
- Communication
- Motor
- Pre-academic
- Leisure/recreational
- Vocational

Self-care skills are generally considered to be of major concern to parents of severely handicapped children. The skills in this area are as important as any in enabling the individual to function in and be accepted by the more normal community. Without such skills, the individual may be ostracized from the "mainstream." Self-care includes such general skills as feeding, toileting, grooming, and dressing.

Socialization has as its major goal the development of skills that will make severely handicapped individuals more acceptable to those around them. Such children often exhibit behaviors that are offensive to others, especially if the handicap involves emotional disturbances. Screaming, grabbing others, self-stimulation, and removal of articles of clothing are not uncommon actions.

Skills typically found in the area of socialization relate to developing interpersonal skills and reducing mal-adaptive behaviors. Examples of these skills include: controlling tantrums, sharing with others, taking turns, eliminating yelling or aggression toward others, and using manners in public.

A less common focus of socialization skills is sex education. The best approach in this area is to involve the parents fully in planning such programs. It is from their concerns that the teacher will develop the most viable curriculum.

Communication requires giving and receiving information. Without these skills, humans are severely restricted in their ability to interact meaningfully with others. Severely handicapped children are often unresponsive to those around them.

With such children, it is necessary to begin at the most basic levels of communication.

Sometimes a child is so deficient that the beginning point is "attention" training, where the child learns to attend to the trainer so that instruction may begin.

Reinforcement of sounds the child spontaneously makes, or attempts to make in imitation of others, is common practice among communication disorders specialists. This training proceeds from imitation of simple sounds to the use of two and/or three word utterances. Most programs train receptive as well as expressive language. Although there is some disagreement among language specialists, many feel that new communication exercises should be as functional as possible in training sessions. With certain children, alternate communication systems must be used, such as sign language with the hearing impaired, or communication boards with cerebral palsied.

Though the degree of motor development varies among the severely handicapped from little or no delay to severe delay and motor pathology, it is common for most of these children to have significant motor problems.

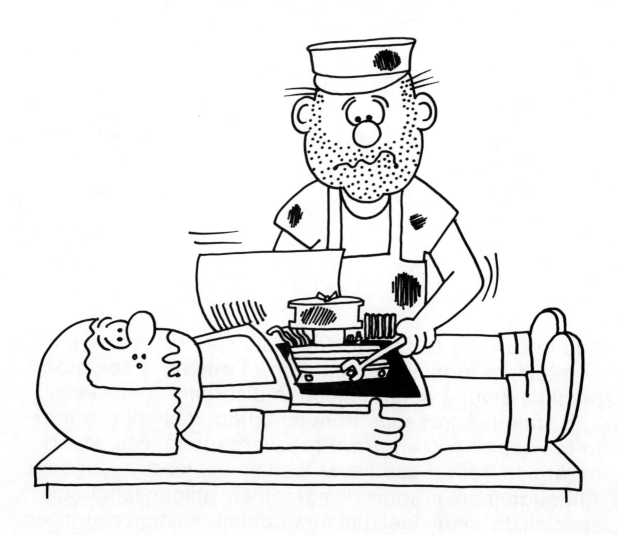

Reasons for many of these delays include brain damage, lack of ability to imitate more normal peers, and central nervous system problems.

Motor skills are generally divided into the areas of gross and fine motor development. When selecting a curriculum for either of these two areas, the teacher should seek one which elicits motor behaviors for functional activities—those things that achieve a useful end as opposed to a meaningless rote exercise.

The program should also accommodate a wide variety of children. It should have criterion measures and be stated in behavioral terms with small steps between items.

When working with children who are cerebral palsied, the teacher will be working with extensive motor problems that may prevent the child from being able to walk, hold the head erect, grasp objects, or control voice. Some children have a problem with over-reactive muscles; others have under-reactive muscles. Various apparatus are available to assist the child in maintaining certain postures. "Standing boxes" and "prone boards" are two examples of such devices.

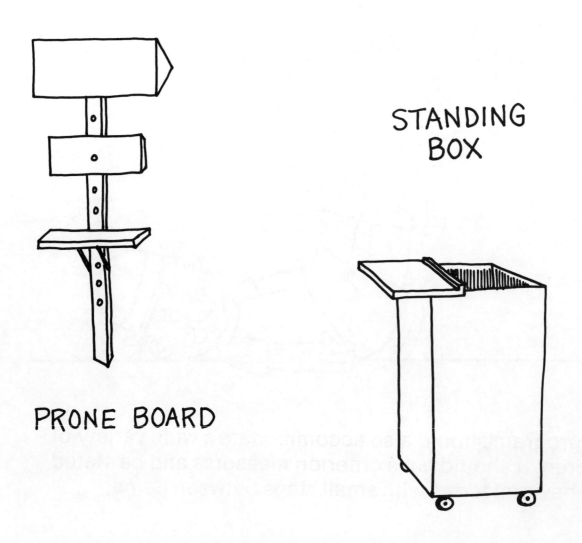

STANDING BOX

PRONE BOARD

Though many severely handicapped children will not progress far enough to move into academic instruction, it is possible that *pre-academic skills* will be important. Attending to task, for example, is a skill that may enable a child to profit from instruction in other areas. In the same way, following simple commands would be important to a child.

Other pre-academic skills are: matching objects, knowing positional prepositions (under, over, in, etc.), identifying objects, and performing simple sorting tasks. Training in these areas should lead to clearly useful ends, and not be "purely academic."

Leisure-recreation skills may, as time passes, prove to be one of the most important areas for severely handicapped individuals.

Though there is considerable emphasis on vocational skills, economic factors like the generally high unemployment rate may make it very unlikely that the severely handicapped will hold jobs in sheltered workshops or other supervised settings. It is much more likely that the severely handicapped will have endless hours of "free time."

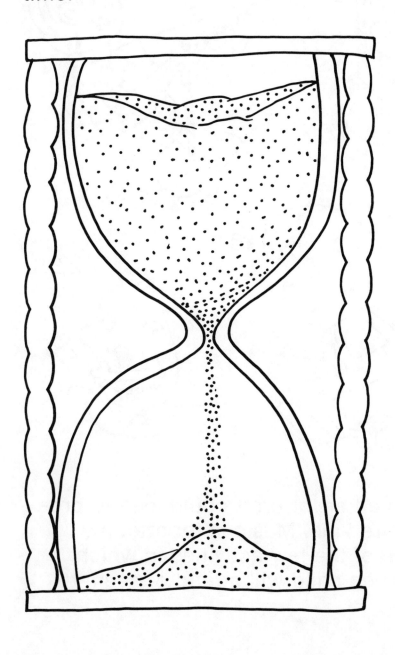

There's nothing to do !

Since the theme in this book has been functional skills, it is much more likely that leisure skills will be more useful than vocational skills. The ability to play simple games, engage in physical activities, raise plants, . . .

. . .pursue a hobby, . . .

. . .or involve oneself in an art or craft could lead to productive, rewarding leisure time. Music is reported by many parents to be one of the few activities to which their severely handicapped child will attend or seem to enjoy.

CURRICULA PROGRAMS

There are a number of well developed curricula available. Various programs divide and label their major component parts in different ways, yet most have primarily the same components that were previously discussed, e.g., self-care, communication, motor skills, pre-academics, and leisure-recreation skills. Listed below are several curricula that teachers may wish to consider.

- *The Data-Based Classroom* by Fredericks, et. al.
- *Systematic Instruction for Retarded Children: The Illinois Program* by Chalfant and Silikovitz.
- *The Portage Guide to Early Education* by Shearer.
- *Learning Accomplishments Profile*
- *Basic Skills Remediation—Manual and Test* by Shalock, Ross and Ross.
- *Teaching Moderately and Severely Handicapped* by Bender and Valletutti.
- *Zero Reject Project Curriculum* by Brown, Scheuerman, Cartwright and York.
- *The Washington State Cooperative Curriculum* by Edgar, et. al.

Vocational and pre-vocational skills should not be ruled out. The severely handicapped have demonstrated the ability to perform productive work such as assembly tasks and other "piece work" in sheltered workshop settings and other training centers. Particularly in periods of favorable economic conditions, there are work options for the severely handicapped. Useful work skills might include assembly, sorting, stuffing envelopes, and folding. Such behaviors as starting on cue, staying on task, not interrupting other workers, and cleaning up work areas are examples of skills which complement the work skills taught.

chapter 3

---

teaching strategies

The evidence is convincing that there are no children who cannot learn at some rate under appropriate environmental conditions. Using the right teaching principles at the right time can lead to the development, reduction, or generalization of behavior. Much of our knowledge about learning abilities of the severely handicapped comes from careful, daily measurements of their performance by teachers and parents. This chapter presents some of these basic teaching principles and on-going measurement procedures. Procedures presented in this chapter are:

- Reinforcement of desired behavior
- Consequences that decrease a behavior
- Over-correction
- Extinction
- Reinforcement of incompatible behaviors
- Time-out
- Shaping
- Training for generalization
- On-going data collection
- Task analysis

BEHAVIORAL PRINCIPLES

Several behavioral principles have come into common use during the last decade. These principles have had the effect of removing the blame for failure from the child and placing it more on the environment. A basic principle is that behavior which is followed by pleasant consequences will tend to increase in rate or maintain itself at its present level. It is said that pleasant consequences *reinforce* a behavior.

Typically, normally growing children are naturally reinforced. Severely handicapped children are not naturally reinforced. Either because of deficiencies in sensory or physical development, they are denied the normal reinforcements available to most children. The child's interaction with the environment is greatly restricted. Consequently, the teacher needs to systematically provide reinforcement. Some severely handicapped children have unusual reinforcement preferences. They may seek activities like flushing toilets or have a strong interest in rubber bands. In the case of edible reinforcers, they may have a specific brand name preference.

With severely handicapped children, there are often times when the need is not to increase a behavior, but rather to decrease it. As was pointed out in the BEH definition, some engage in behavioral excesses. In these cases, it may be necessary to provide a consequence that reduces a behavior. The technical term is punishment.

It involves the direct presentation of an aversive stimulus. Such a procedure should not be used until other more positive approaches have been tried or unless the behavior presents the likelihood of harm to the child or others.

Overcorrection is a commonly used procedure to reduce the occurrence of an undesired behavior. There are two approaches to overcorrection. The first is restitution, in which the person is made to correct the results of his behavior. For the child who paints on the wall, the requirement might be to clean up the paint plus wash the entire wall. At times it is necessary to force the person through each of the cleaning up motions.

Another form of overcorrection requires that positive practice be repeated several times in order to get the child to practice the correct behavior. Making a child close the door correctly several times is an example of this procedure.

Another approach to reducing behavior is to withhold reinforcement from undesired behaviors. This is referred to as extinction. Behavior that is not reinforced will, in all likelihood, reduce in frequency. Adult attention is very reinforcing to most children. The removal of that attention is a powerful technique which can result in reducing or eliminating undesired behavior. Unfortunately, children often get more attention for their undesired behavior than for their desired behavior.

Ignoring a temper tantrum is often effective in eliminating it. Ignoring non-verbal communications can result in reduction of non-verbal attempts with a subsequent increase of vocalizations. Ignoring misbehaviors may cause them to disappear. Keep in mind that some behaviors cannot be safely ignored since the child or others may get hurt as a result.

A reaction that teachers and parents need to watch for is the child's increased effort when the behavior is first ignored. Often the behavior gets worse until, after a few days, the child sees that reinforcement definitely will not be forthcoming.

Another way of reducing a behavior is to reinforce an incompatible behavior. By reinforcing a desirable, incompatible behavior, the undesired behavior is unlikely to occur.

For example, reinforcing swallowing makes drooling less likely to occur because swallowing is incompatible with drooling. Increasing sharing of toys reduces the likelihood of taking toys. Reinforcing socialization reduces the possibilities for isolated behavior.

Time-out is a way of reducing behavior which is accomplished by removing the child from a reinforcing situation. When the child is misbehaving in class or is aggressive toward a peer on the playground, it may be appropriate to remove the child from the situation for a brief period.

TIME OUT
AREA

A "chair time-out" at the side of the classroom sometimes suffices. At other times, it is necessary to com-
pletely remove the individual from the setting. It is
important that no reinforcing consequences be present.
One procedure is to remove the child to the time-out
area for a specific amount of time, such as five minutes.
Another is to remove the child for a specific amount of
time which begins *after* the more appropriate behavior
starts. For example, you may say to the child, "You may
return to class five minutes after you stop screaming."

Time-out, like punishment, is often abused. Children should not be placed in such situations for long periods of time. There is no evidence that long periods of time-out are more effective than brief periods. Children should not be placed in time-out until other less intrusive methods have been tried. In addition, they should have supervision at all times.

It may be possible to increase or decrease behaviors by using the procedures discussed above, but the teacher must be careful not to proceed too rapidly. Severely handicapped children need to move in a slow, but deliberate manner from one skill to the next. Shaping is a procedure used for moving the child through small steps or successive approximations to a terminal goal.

To illustrate, a child who is learning to dress may not be expected initially to independently complete any part of dressing, requiring complete assistance from the teacher in putting on a coat. This could be called a full physical prompt. Later, the child may be expected to get the coat into position, but need help in putting both arms through the sleeves and buttoning the coat. This could be called a partial physical prompt. As the child learns to do most of the steps, needing only a few gestural and verbal cues, we can say the behavior of "putting-on-coat" has been gradually shaped into the child's repertoire.

In shaping new skills, many teachers use the *levels of assistance* previously mentioned—that is, physical prompt, gestural prompt, and verbal prompt. In the process of shaping a new behavior these cues are *faded.* Fading is a process of removing a stimulus or a cue very slowly so that it takes a smaller cue to elicit the desired behavior.

1.
2.

In the dressing example, the child would initially be given physical, gestural, and verbal cues on all trials. Eventually, cues would be *faded* until only the verbal cue would be necessary. Another example of fading is the case in which the teacher gradually erases the dotted lines around the correct answer to a problem.

A procedure used by many teachers of the severely handicapped is chaining—moving from one behavior to the next in a sequence of skills. Both forward and reverse chaining are possible. Forward chaining is most appropriate for teaching skills that are developmental, like walking. Reverse chaining is often used to teach skills that involve self-care. Reverse chaining requires the child to perform the last behavior in a sequence, like pulling the bow tight on a shoestring. On the next trial, the last two steps are performed, and so on until the child can start at the beginning and complete all steps in the new skill.

Regardless of the skill being taught, the teacher should always train for generalization of the new behavior. Teach the child to perform the skill in the settings of most importance. We often forget that the "real world" for a child is outside the classroom. Training for generalization is critical for severely handicapped children. While normal children typically generalize new skills to out-of-class settings without intervention, we cannot expect severely handicapped children to do this.

One way to increase the probability of generalization is to arrange the training setting so that it closely resembles the setting in which the child is expected to perform. Making the classroom more like a home or work setting enhances the amount of generalization. Training in several different settings should increase generalization across situations.

It is likely that using more than one trainer will increase generalization, especially across trainers. Another way to teach generalization is to teach many different instances of the same skill, for example to teach a child all of the forms of a food that are appropriate to eat (boiled, fried, scrambed and poached egg). Don't expect it; train for it.

DATA COLLECTION

In Chapter 2, long-term assessment was discussed. On-going assessment or measurement is included in Chapter 3 since it is so closely tied to the instructional process.

Programs for the severely handicapped are often data-based. That means teachers are making instructional decisions on the basis of direct, daily measurement of pupil behaviors.

Taking daily measurement of important behaviors helps teachers detect changes in behaviors that may have otherwise gone unnoticed. With the severely handicapped this is especially true. Child changes are often not readily apparent because they may be slight or subtle, or because of teacher bias. Taking data also provides information about where the child began which can later be used to compare child performance. Data collected on a regular basis allows the teacher to be very accountable. It can demonstrate to parents and others that changes specified in the Individualized Instructional Plan for the child were made.

The on-going data collection procedures discussed in this chapter are those originally outlined by Vance Hall (1971). The first of these is automatic recording techniques. This requires the use of mechanical or electro-mechanical devices that automatically record information. An example is a counter placed on a wheel chair which records the number of revolutions the wheel has made during a specified time period.

Another automatic procedure is the use of a tape recorder having a voice operated switch, which enables it to run only when sound is present. Though convenient and accurate, these devices are limited by the number of behaviors with which they may be used.

A second procedure is to record behavior through the use of permanent products. Many behaviors naturally leave a permanent record which can easily be counted, such as the number of smoked cigarettes left in an ashtray.

Unbuttoned buttons provide a partial record of a child's independent dressing skills. Coats on the floor, food on the plate, wet pants, and math problems on the paper are all permanent products that can be counted by the teacher after the behavior has occurred.

A third approach is to use a human observer who is trained to make judgments about whether the behavior of concern occurred. The simplest procedure is to record events. The observer simply tallies the number of times the child is seen engaging in the target behavior. This technique works well for behaviors that are discretely occurring events, like number of hands raised, children present, and words or sounds uttered. It does not work well for behaviors that might occur for varying periods of time, such as crying or tantrums.

Duration recording is well suited for collecting information on occurrence of behaviors that may be exhibited for different lengths of time. Duration measurements require the observer to time rather than to tally specific behaviors. The amount of time spent in water play,...

...the length of time exercising, and the seconds required to grasp an object are examples of behaviors that are best recorded by the duration method.

Interval recording is useful for collecting data when the teacher is unable to continuously observe for a longer period of time. The teacher can divide the day into thirty blocks or intervals. At the end of each interval, the teacher records the occurrences of the behavior(s). Attention to task, involvement in free play . . .

. . .and lying in a prone position are all examples of behaviors that can be recorded using the interval system.

Occasionally a teacher may be interested in latency, which is simply the time between two events. For example, a teacher may wish to know how long a child typically takes to respond to a verbal cue, or to turn to a sound. The time recorded between the onset of the cue and the response of the child would be the latency measurement.

Each of the recording procedures discussed on the preceding pages has its advantages and limitations. It is up to the teacher to select the most appropriate procedure or technique. Selection considerations include: the behavior of concern, the setting, and the resources available.

TASK ANALYSIS

Teaching severely handicapped children new skills usually requires that in addition to the use of effective behavioral principles, the teacher carefully program the complexity and sequence of skills to be learned. These children need small, clearly stated steps, as discussed earlier in the section on shaping.

Task analysis is the procedure used to develop efficient skill sequences for shaping new behaviors.

The first step in the process is to determine the behavioral objective or terminal behaviors; that is, what do you want the child to end up doing? A well-stated behavioral objective should include a statement of the observable skill the child should attain, the level of performance expected, and the conditions under which the skill should be performed.

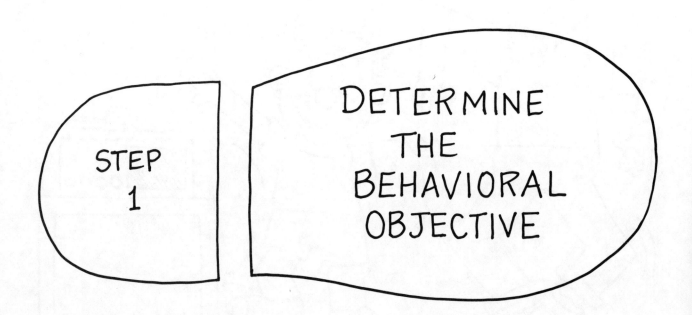

STEP 1

DETERMINE THE BEHAVIORAL OBJECTIVE

Second, the teacher needs to identify the sequence of skills leading to the terminal behavior. The size of the steps a task is divided into is relatively arbitrary as there is no set formula for doing this. For severely handicapped children, however, the smaller the steps, the better. One way to divide the task is while watching an adult or child perform the task, record in writing each discernable step in the sequence. A new step can usually be identified when the direction of movement changes. Another way to determine a sequence is to seek information from "expert" sources like child development specialists or textbooks.

STEP 2

IDENTIFY SEQUENCE OF SKILLS

Third, identify the entry behaviors necessary, i.e., what does the child need to know or do as a prerequisite skill? What specific motor, verbal, cognitive, or social skills are required as a basis for learning the new behavior? If a listing of prerequisite or entry skills is overlooked, the teacher may miss important behaviors that will prevent the child from successfully performing the new behavior.

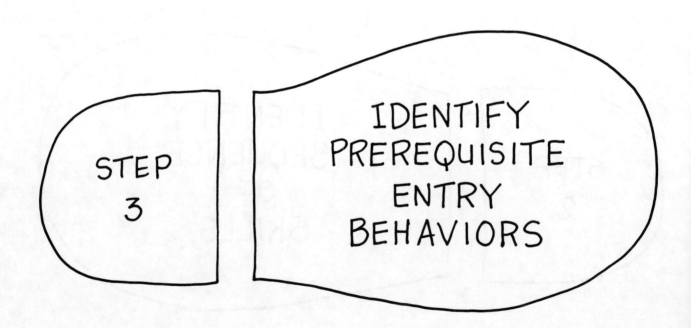

STEP 3

IDENTIFY PREREQUISITE ENTRY BEHAVIORS

Finally, determine the order in which you plan to teach the sub-tasks. The two main approaches are forward and reverse chaining, as were discussed earlier. The entire process could be diagrammed like this:

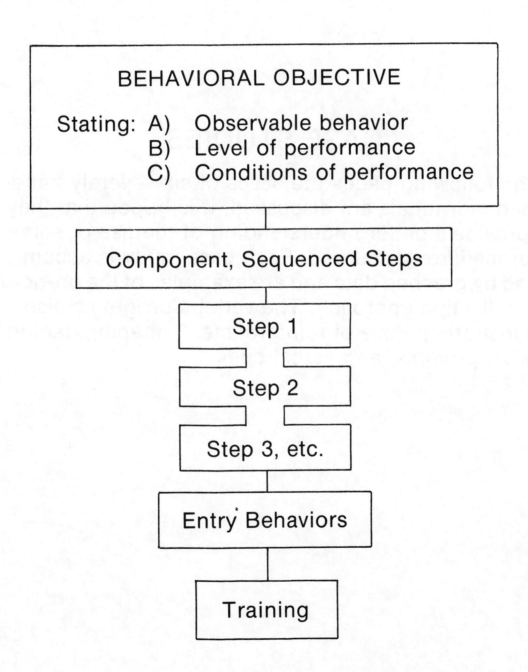

CASE STUDIES

On the following pages the cases of six severely handicapped individuals are discussed. It is hoped that they
will provide a better understanding of the use of some of
the procedures discussed. Each case study is accom-
panied by graphed data and are examples of the on-going
data collection approach. The various programs also
demonstrate the use of reinforcement, shaping, fading,
physical prompts, and verbal cues.

SHERI

Sheri is a six-year-old multiply handicapped girl. She is considered severely retarded, legally deaf and blind, and has a seizure disorder. Generally, she is functioning below one year developmentally.

The teacher is working with Sheri on many self-care tasks and teaching her to respond to environmental cues and simple directions. One task Sheri is working on is putting rings on and taking them off a ring tree. Sheri showed fairly rapid acquisition of the skill of taking rings off, as shown in Figure 1. However, the task of placing rings on, required much more careful planning and instruction on the part of the teacher. During the first condition, without physical prompts, Sheri made no measurable progress. During the second condition the teacher provided the physical prompt of lifting Sheri's arm at the elbow until she successfully removed each ring. In just two weeks Sheri reached the criterion of 100% correct, but remember that was with considerable prompting. During the third phase the teacher lifted Sheri's elbow only to table level, leaving Sheri to complete the movement on her own. Notice in Figure 2 the significant drop in Sheri's performance when this condition was implemented, but the rapid recovery to criterion. The next step in the sequence will be to further fade the physical prompt so Sheri can independently perform the task.

SUBJECT: Sheri
BEHAVIOR: to remove rings

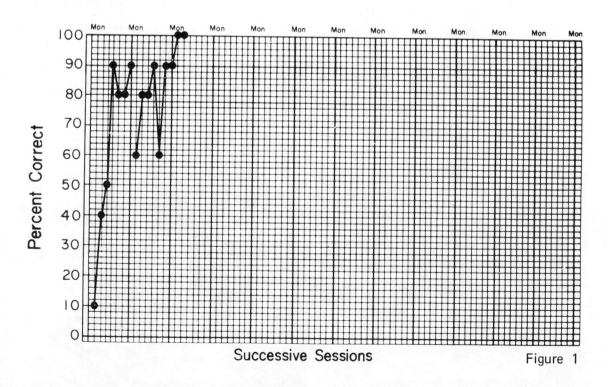

Successive Sessions

Figure 1

105

SUBJECT: Sheri
BEHAVIOR: to place rings on

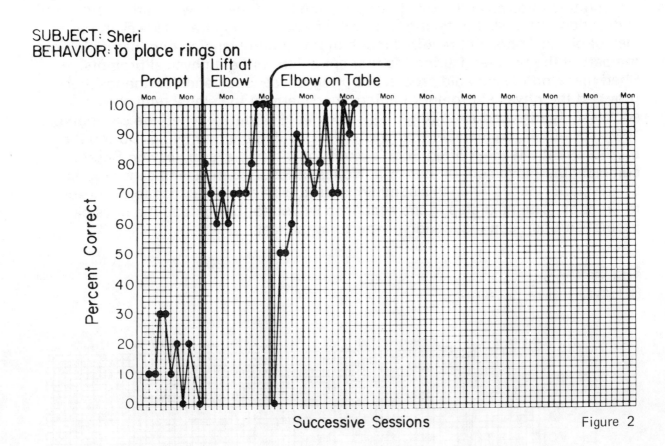

Figure 2

MICHELE

Michele is a profoundly retarded eight-year-old girl with multiple handicaps. She apparently suffered pervasive brain damage as a result of prolonged anoxia. In all areas she is functioning below the one-month level developmentally.

In an effort to develop a consistent response to a verbal cue the teacher and communication disorders specialist decided to say, "Hi, Michele" at intermittent times and reinforce Michele by tickling if she looked at the speaker. Because of scheduling difficulties the program was conducted mainly during a brief period in the afternoon. When the teachers began to distribute the trials throughout the day as shown in Figure 3, Michele's proportion of response to the cue increased dramatically.

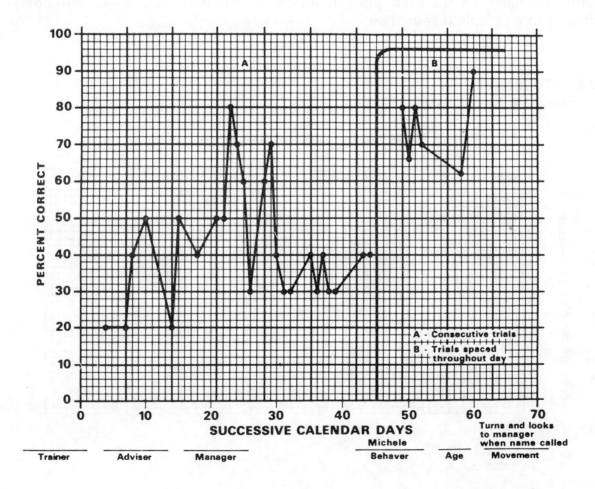

Figure 3

JOHN

John is a 21-year-old young man with Down's Syndrome who functions near the three-year-old level, except in language where he functions at about the 18-month-level.

In teaching John some vocational tasks the manager found that he had to teach very small components of a task to 100% accuracy before advancing to the next component. For example, in assembling flour sifters, a small relatively simple task, the manager taught John to correctly place some mechanical rods to 100% accuracy (see Figure 4). When John had mastered that step he progressed to placement of the sifting screens, which again took several days to master. Finally, the manager combined these and some previously taught steps to assemble a complete unit. As seen in condition three, it took several weeks for John to achieve 100% correct performance when the individual steps were combined into a complete sequence.

SUBJECT: John
BEHAVIOR: to assemble parts of flour sifter

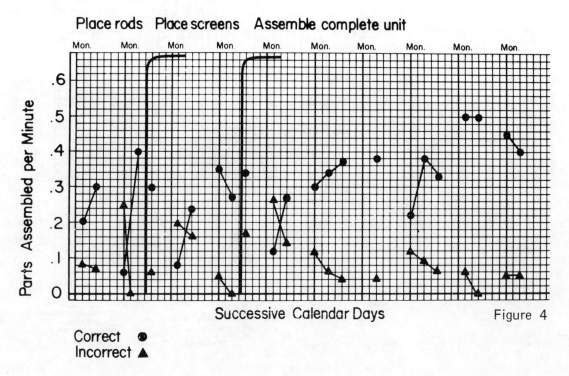

Figure 4

Correct ●
Incorrect ▲

SHEREEN

Shereen is an 18-year-old emotionally disturbed, severely retarded girl. In the pre-vocational classroom she was being taught to assemble a pulley. The task was taught by component parts. As can be seen in Figure 5, Shereen demonstrated good progress and reached the criterion of 80% on correct placement of a chain, and consolidated the first five pieces of the pulley assembly. However, on the next step, placement of a large hex nut which is used to hold the pulley together, Shereen failed to make the same degree of progress. Our efforts to teach this step to Shereen currently consist of providing increased prompts and physical assistance in correctly placing the hex nut.

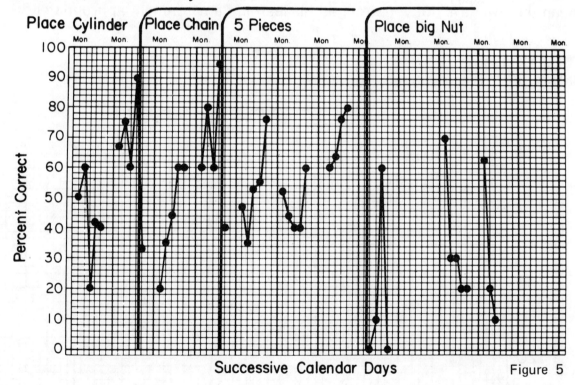

SUBJECT: Shereen
BEHAVIOR: to assemble Pulley Parts

Figure 5

LLOYD

Lloyd is a five-and-one-half-year-old boy enrolled in a classroom for "severely emotionally disturbed" children. He exhibits no expressive language, has very little social interaction and engages in a variety of self-stimulatory behaviors. In all areas he functions developmentally between the first and second year, with a few "splinter" skills at higher levels.

One of the tasks the teacher selected was placement of four forms, a square, circle, triangle, and rectangle, in their appropriate slots in a form board. For each correct placement Lloyd was given a raisin, coupled with teacher praise. After three weeks the teacher noted no notable decrease of errors or increase of correct placement. Then she began to use the raisin as a cue as well as a reinforcer; she pointed to the correct space with the raisin then gave it to Lloyd when he correctly placed a form. Even then Lloyd's errors remained high. However, when the teacher simplified the task so that Lloyd had only to place a square and circle in the form board, his errors did decline. These data, shown in Figure 6, exemplify the point that the failure of a pupil to show progress may mean that we have not yet arranged his learning environment appropriately.

SUBJECT: Lloyd
BEHAVIOR: to place shape in formboard

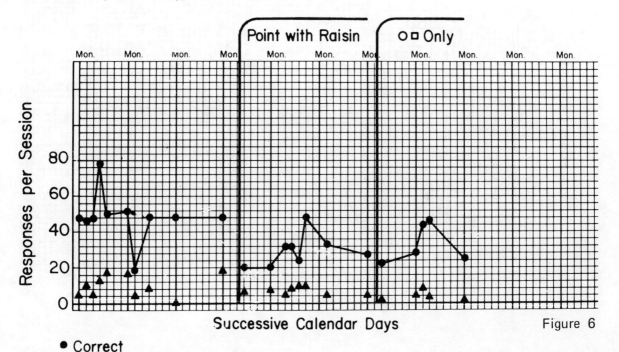

Figure 6

• Correct
▲ Incorrect

ROY

Roy is a nine-year-old boy considered deaf, blind, and severely retarded, probably resulting from rubella. In all developmental areas he is functioning between five and ten month levels.

Since there was no discernable physical reason why Roy should not learn to walk, it was one of the tasks selected for instruction. The teacher further selected cruising (i.e. walking sideways holding onto something) left to right and right to left as the initial task. The criterion for success was a total of 50 correct steps per day, taken without physical assistance from the teacher. When Roy could complete this criterion around a selected table with the classroom, as shown in Figure 7, his practice sessions were moved to a new location within the classroom and the teacher began taking frequency data during a one-minute sample. Roy practiced cruising for several days in the classroom and soon reached a criterion of ten steps per minute in both directions. At this time his sessions were moved to a rail located along the hallway outside his classroom. Upon the transition, his right to left performance showed no appreciable decrease but his left to right performance did show a decrease. Within three weeks, however, Roy was able to cruise at forty steps per minute in either direction (see Figure 8).

SUBJECT: Roy
BEHAVIOR: Steps

Right to Left

Left to Right

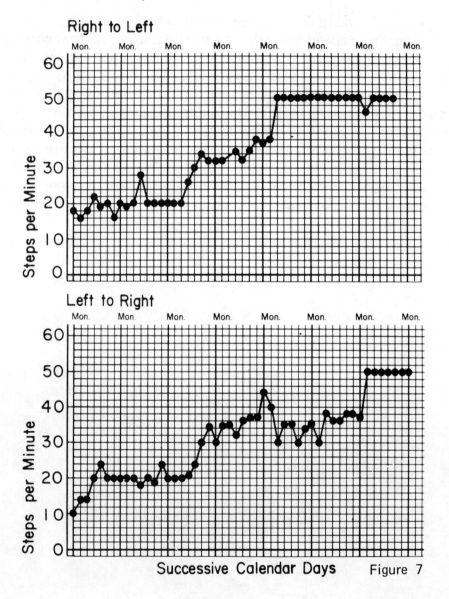

Successive Calendar Days   Figure 7

SUBJECT: Roy
BEHAVIOR: Steps

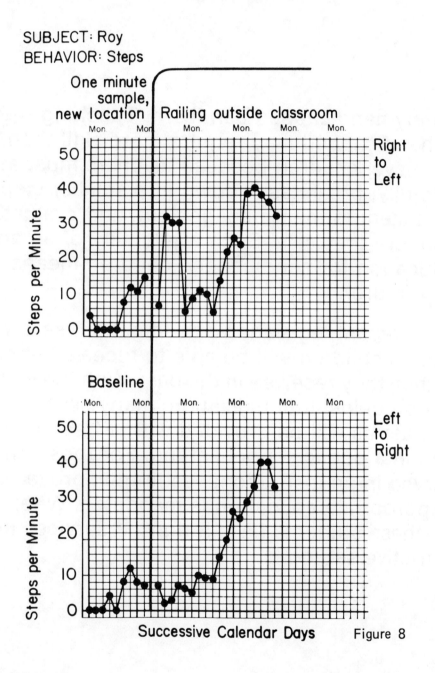

Figure 8

The severely handicapped *can* learn. Teaching the severely handicapped may require more skill than teaching higher level children because teachers must assess more carefully, break tasks down into smaller steps, be more consistent in their management, and evaluate progress more precisely. Such availability of an appropriate education for handicapped children means a more promising future.

Because of recent legislation and litigation, severely handicapped children will be able to receive better services than they received in the past. With the increased emphasis on deinstitutionalization, many severely handicapped students will be provided with a free, appropriate education in a public school setting. For those children being served in an institutional setting, improved services and an appropriate education is mandated. Wherever they are, these students have a right to services in the least restrictive setting.

BIBLIOGRAPHY

Hall, V. Managing behavior, Part I, behavior modification: the measurement of behavior. Lawrence, Kansas: H & H Enterprises, 1971.

York, R., & Edgar, E. Teaching the severely handicapped: an annual publication of the American Association for the Education of the Severely/Profoundly Handicapped, Volume Four. Bexley, Ohio: Special Press, 1977, in press.

About the Authors

Currently, Dale Gentry is Associate Professor of Education in the area of special education at the University of Idaho. Dr. Gentry earned his Ph.D. at the University of Washington. He has served as Chief Administrator and Principal of the Experimental Education Unit and as the Project Manager for the Program to Provide Services to Severely Handicapped Children and Youth, both at the University of Washington.

A. Lee Parks is an Associate Professor of Special Education at the University of Idaho. He began his professional career as a school psychologist in the state of Washington. He attended the University of Kansas where he received his Ph.D. During this time he worked as a Research Trainee for the Bureau of Child Research. After receiving his doctorate he accepted a position at The Ohio State University where he held a joint appointment with the Nisonger Center for Mental Retardation and the Faculty for Exceptional Children. He is presently at the University of Idaho.

About the Illustrator

Everyone can draw—some with more competence than others. Occasionally you find someone who is exceptionally gifted in a particular facet of drawing. Danial B. Fairchild is that someone. He is a highly talented cartoonist with a style that is uniquely his own. His achievements include cartoons printed in newspapers and magazines, and most recently two paperbacks entitled **Cowtoons** (Artcraft Press, Nampa, Idaho), which depict in a very humorous way, the life of cowboys.